# Becoming *Her*

## Purpose Journal

## For Fearless Women

Dr. Sherrie Walton

Walton Publishing House
Copyright © 2022 by  Dr. Sherrie Walton

Reviewers may quote brief passages in reviews.
Walton Publishing House
Houston, Texas
www.waltonpublishinghouse.com
Printed in the United States of America

Disclaimer: The advice found within may not be suitable for every individual. This work is purchased with the understanding that neither the author nor the publisher are held responsible for any results. Neither author nor publisher assumes responsibility for errors, omissions, or contrary interpretations of the subject matter herein. Any perceived disparagement of an individual or organization is a misinterpretation.
Brand and product names mentioned are trademarks that belong solely to their respective owners.

Library of Congress Cataloging-in-Publication Data under
ISBN: 978-1-953993-63-2

*This journal belongs to*

_____

She is a woman of purpose, value, worth, charisma, uniqueness, and intelligence. She is loved by all who meet her, favored by those who know her, and most importantly, she is becoming a woman of purpose.

"A capable, intelligent, and virtuous woman—who is he who can find her? She is far more precious than jewels and her value is far above rubies or pearls."

Proverbs 31:10 AMPC

# Contents

*Hello Beautiful!*

# Contents

# Hello Beautiful!

Are you ready to live a life filled with purpose? Well, don't answer that question just yet. I want us to spend some time together getting to know more about each other before we get too personal so soon.

I'll go first.

Hi, I am Sherrie. I am an introvert with extrovert tendencies who discovered my purpose-filled life in my late thirties after being stuck in unhealthy life cycles for more than 10 years. I had no idea who I was, and I was fearful. Of what? Glad you asked! Fearful of my gift, fearful of other people's opinions, fearful of accepting my public flaws and shortcomings, and fearful of being too successful (crazy, I know). For years I gave others the power over my voice. I was concerned about what they thought of me as I wrestled with imposter syndrome.

It was a long journey to the rediscovery of me. Today I can boldly say that the broken little girl no longer lives here. I will never forget the lessons that shaped me into the woman of God I am today. For the past seven years, I have been helping other women like you also rediscover themselves.

Over the next 31 days, you and I will embark on the journey to fulfilling your purpose and God-given assignment through journaling. Spending quiet time and journaling is an excellent way for you to connect with your true self and align your spirit to receive direction. The truth is journaling saved my life. I don't mean this figuratively but literally. Incorporating journaling into my healing, restoration, and redemption journey birthed my purpose. I believe it will do the same for you. At least, that is my prayer and expectation as you work your way through this journal. I won't keep you much longer, so let's dive in.

●●●●●●●●●●●●●●●●●●●●●●●●●●●●●●●●●●●●●●●●●●●●▶

Who Are You?

$\mathcal{S}$itting on the island of Barbados and overlooking the beach off my balcony, I feel free, happy, and connected to God. The sound of the ocean always causes me to sit and think about my beginning. It makes me reflect on my journey to purpose. I believe many women have difficulty discovering their purpose because they forget about the things that make them feel connected to themselves. They forget how to connect with their foundation.

Today, connect to who God created you to be.

Do you remember who you are? Do you remember what makes you feel connected, happy, and free? Do you know what makes you stand out from others? What makes your voice unique? At the core of you, what gives brings you peace? What makes you feel like a woman? These seem like simple questions, right? Unfortunately, as women, we often become so many things to everyone else that we morph into someone we no longer recognize. We bury the beauty of who we are; spending so much time serving others and putting their needs before ours that we lose ourselves.

So, who are you? I don't mean the labels of Mom, Wife, CEO, Corporate Leader, Spiritual Leader... but who are you? On the journey of purpose, this is your first stop. Clarity about who you are helps you gain clarity on why you have been placed on this earth. You were created for something extraordinary; do you believe it?

# Journal Activity:

Reflect on the questions above and write the answers below. After you have written them down, close your eyes and see yourself being the best version. See yourself being the true woman that God created you to be. You're a fearless woman, loved and validated by her Father in Heaven. Can you see her yet?

# Journal Here:

_____

_____

_____

_____

_____

_____

_____

_____

_____

_____

_____

# Be Free, Be You!

*A* bird landed on my table while sitting at my favorite outdoor restaurant. I sat there eating my breakfast overlooking the balcony as he (or she) made their way into my space. It landed on my table and stared at me. We sat there peering at each other, wondering who would make the first move. Then, seconds later, I watched it fly to my balcony railing, down to the ground, and back up again. It was as if it was saying, hey, look at me. The bird was so free and unbothered by me watching it.

Observing that bird at that moment prompted me to think about how differently that scenario would have been if that were another woman. My curious observation of her probably would have made her self-conscious of her movements. My stares surely would have made her behave differently. Having all eyes on us sometimes makes us shrink and the attention can limit our ability to move freely.

We live in a society where validation and acceptance are overrated. People are very judgmental, and their judgments often limit us from moving forward. Fear of being judged stunts our growth, and before long, we are afraid of being "too much" or "not enough" in the eyes of others. But think about how freeing it is to be who you are no matter who is watching you.

Don't allow the opinions of others to limit you from moving forward. Don't allow the stares and commentary to keep you from soaring. Be free to express yourself whether all eyes are on you or you're in a room by yourself. It doesn't matter. Be free to be you!

# Journal Activity:

Reflect on an area in your life where the opinions of others have limited you. Write a statement to yourself that frees your mind from the place of limiting beliefs.

# Journal Here:

# Your Journey to Purpose

*H*ave you ever asked yourself, what is my purpose? I remember the first time that question popped into my mind. My life was falling apart, and I didn't know where to look to discover it. My second attempt at owning a business failed, and I was in so much debt. I was embarrassed and I hid from the shame and guilt for almost a full year. My world was chaotic, and I was too prideful to let anyone know I needed help.

How could all this drama happen to a good person like me? I asked. Failure sucks, but oftentimes it redirects us to our purpose. I wish someone had warned me about this. I had no idea that failure would lead me to my purpose. I later learned that many people have at least one story in their past that they wish could be erased from their story. Truly successful individuals courageously fight through their difficult times. Purpose is experienced by those that persevere against all odds to become who God created them to be.

Looking back over those situations that were such a blow to my gut at the time, I can now see the lessons. I can clearly see what I needed to learn about myself.

But, most importantly, what I needed to learn about God. What lessons have you learned about yourself on your journey to purpose?

# Journal Activity:

Reflect and write what comes to mind when you think about your journey to purpose. Write the setbacks you have experienced and what lessons you learned from them.

# Journal Here:

_____

_____

_____

_____

_____

_____

_____

_____

_____

_____

_____

_____

A Woman of Purpose

*W*hen God created you, He started with your purpose in mind. He knew you would be here at this moment and intricately crafted you so the world would need what you have on the inside of you. A woman that knows her purpose and lives a life of purpose is not moved by the challenges that life brings. In fact, a woman of purpose is so focused on creating a life God intended for her that she doesn't allow herself to be affected by what she sees in the natural world. She is focused and determined and clear about the path to follow.

Jeremiah 1:5 (NIV) says, "Before I formed you in the womb I knew you, before you were born, I set you apart." I remember the first time I read that and the feeling that overtook me. It was a promising glimmer of hope that brought light to one of the darkest moments of my life. Maybe God could still use me even after everything I had done and everything I had endured. Maybe my pain wasn't the end of my story. It was then I knew I had a purpose.

A woman that understands her purpose understands that she is valuable and worthy.

In case life has seemingly told you otherwise, I want you to know that you have purpose and it's time for you to fearlessly walk into it. Don't get caught up in the how, just know that God handpicked you before you entered this world. He knew you would be great.

# Journal Activity:

Reflect on Jeremiah 1:5. How does reading these words make you feel? Write what this scripture means to you and how does it impact your understanding of your purpose?

# Journal Here:

_____

_____

_____

_____

_____

_____

_____

_____

_____

_____

_____

_____

# Loving Yourself

*I* have been called the "Midwife of Purpose" by my sisters in the faith. With this title comes the responsibility of helping as many women as I can birth their purpose. It is my duty to hold up the "imaginary mirror" and ask you, what do you see? If any negative thoughts enter your mind - we have some work to do. I am on an assignment to arrest any thoughts you have about yourself that are contrary to the Word of God.

His word says you're fearfully and wonderfully made, and that you're made in His image and likeness. Think about how beautifully He sees you; now accept that you are perfect just the way you are. When I was a little girl, my mother often said, "God doesn't make any junk. She was right.

You are priceless...
You are a masterpiece...
You are a designer's original...

When was the last time you looked in the mirror and smiled at what you saw? Loving yourself is loving all of you. It's looking at what God sees and coming in agreement with what He says.

# Journal Activity:

Take a moment to see yourself the way that God sees you.
Reflect on what He says about you. What are some of the
things you need to release to start loving yourself the way
God wants you to?

# Journal Here:

_____

_____

_____

_____

_____

_____

_____

_____

_____

_____

_____

Blurred Vision

*If* you are an eyeglass wearer you know firsthand what blurred vision looks like when you are not wearing your spectacles...a fancy word for eyeglasses. Well, maybe you don't wear glasses, but you have gotten something stuck in your eye before and it affected your vision temporarily.

Blurred or temporarily impaired vision will make you lose your focus. Blurred vision can keep you searching for something that's right in front of your face. It can cause you to feel off-balanced and off-centered. Do you recognize that feeling?

Now let's think about how a blurred-life vision can also affect us. When there isn't a clear vision for your life, you will roam aimlessly in the same cycles, doing the same things, with the same people, and getting the same results. I'm sure that's not how you want to live because that can be frustrating and unfulfilling.

Close your eyes and see yourself winning. See yourself victorious in life. See yourself shining brightly and walking in your purpose and helping others to walk in their purpose as well.

What does that look like for you? How does visualizing it make you feel? Those are the emotions that I want you to tap into today and every day forward. Before you become the woman you've been purposed to be, you must clearly see her.

# Journal Activity:

Think about what you really want for your life and write it down. Reflect on your dreams and see yourself becoming her - no matter how big and how frightening it may seem.

# Journal Here:

_____

_____

_____

_____

_____

_____

_____

_____

_____

_____

_____

# Unlimited
## Possibilties

𝒟o you know there are no limits to who you can be in this life? Do you fully understand that you were created as a being with no limitations? Do you ever wonder what your life would be like if you really tapped into who you were created to be?

If you are not living a life of unlimited possibilities, what is stopping you from becoming the person you once dreamed you could be?

- Is it self-sabotage?
- Is it your mindset?
- Is it the stories and struggles of your past?
- Is it your environment?

The person you are today - good or bad- has been shaped by what you thought was possible. It's time for you to go deeper and tap into the full potential of who you are. I want to challenge you to remove the blinders that cause you to play small. I want you to stop rehearsing your past. I want you to stop placing the blame on others. I want you to take accountability and make the commitment that you deserve.

You serve a God that owns everything. Not only is He your God, but He is also your Father. This means that what He owns, you have access to it. You are made in His likeness. Whatever abilities He has, you also have. If your Father owns and has access to everything, what does that say about you?

Take some time today to reflect on what a life of unlimited possibilities looks like for you. Allow the Holy Spirit to reprogram your mindset for unlimited possibilities.

# Journal Activity:

List the limiting beliefs that keep you from living a life of unlimited possibilities. Decide that these beliefs are no longer yours. Release them from your life.

# Journal Here:

_____

_____

_____

_____

_____

_____

_____

_____

_____

_____

_____

Get Unstuck

*I* once stepped on a sticky wad of pink bubble gum and oh! the frustration I immediately felt as I tracked the gum with each step. I was stuck...with a wad of gooey mess on the bottom of my sole. Yuck!

When I analyze our lives, I realize that frustration and being stuck often go hand in hand. Being stuck is that feeling that many people feel when facing a major life change. They stand at the crossroad - leery about the decision that needs to be made in fear of making the wrong one. Many of us have a hard time deciding on what to eat for dinner, let alone knowing what course God wants to lead us on to discover our purpose.

It's not uncommon to have a fear of making the wrong move. In fact, it is fear that keeps many believers making no move at all, and before they realize it, they are sitting in that same place in life for years, stagnant, waiting for a sign. Yes, I remember that feeling all too well. For years I was stuck in the same rut, making little progress hoping to play it safe. After years of rehearsing the same story, I had to be honest with myself and admit I was the only person that would rescue me. As much as I wanted Him to,

Jesus wasn't coming down for a personal visit to help me with the areas I was already equipped with the tools to handle.

Are you stuck? Have you been racking your brain trying to narrow down what path you should take? Don't worry, you're not alone. In fact, 3 out of 10 people admit to feeling stuck in life. They experience the effects of fear when they consider taking the leap of faith to do something they will enjoy–but sadly, they sit and watch and wait for the perfect time, which of course never comes. "I am waiting on God," is what many of them say. My response is always to them, "No, God is waiting on you."

I can give you some of my best suggestions to get you unstuck but unless you decide to move forward, they won't work. The reality is, you're the only one that can unstick yourself. You can attend the best seminars, and read the best books, but until you decide that you are ready to make a move, you will stay where you are for years. You'll be miserable until you give birth to the dream! The answers for your next move lie within you. Are you willing to do the work? Are you ready to experience your next journey?

# Journal Activity:

Today, reflect on the areas you have been stagnant and stuck. Write them down and make a commitment that as of this day you refuse to remain stuck anymore.

# Journal Here:

_____

_____

_____

_____

_____

_____

_____

_____

_____

_____

_____

*H*ave you ever looked at your life and thought, boy, did I royally screw that up? And to make matters worse, after you messed up, you found yourself feeling guilty? Just sit here for a moment. Breathe. You have beat yourself up long enough. It happened and you can't change it.

Don't let the guilt of your past keep you from fulfilling your God-ordained destiny. Can you be honest with yourself and admit that if you had fully forgiven yourself for the mistakes of your past, you would be much further along in life by now? You have given guilt and regret so much power and they have hindered your growth. Isn't it interesting that when you decide that you deserve a better life and you're going to move forward, those toxic areas peep their head up and start whispering contrary thoughts? Unforgiveness is a weight that keeps you tied to the pain of your past. But don't let it keep you back any longer.

What have you put off achieving because you haven't forgiven yourself? Is it finishing that degree? Is it pursuing that business? What about pursuing your dreams?

dreams? Do you allow others room for error, and constantly forgive them but don't extend yourself the same courtesy? Do you beat yourself up about mistakes of your past? Can you forgive yourself? I think you can.

You deserve to live the life of your dreams...no matter what!

# Journal Activity:

Write down the areas where unforgiveness has caused you to live below what God has purposed for you. Make a decision that you will not be held back any longer.

# Journal Here:

_____

_____

_____

_____

_____

_____

_____

_____

_____

_____

_____

_____

Fearless
Leader

Many great women have made an impact on our world with their fearless "can do" approach to life. These women have overcome life's obstacles and pursued their purpose with a fearlessness that transposes from their inner thoughts to their outward actions. They are news and history makers who march to the beat of their drum, and they live their life with a boldness that cannot be silenced.

If you take the time to study them or read their stories, you'll realize they aren't much different from you and me. Some of them rose from the most deplorable living conditions, worse than we could ever imagine. Others built their lives from the bricks thrown at them by others. Their stories may be different but overcoming life's challenges and achieving greatness is something they all have in common.

We all have a story...everyone has been through a life hardship or difficulty. These women realized that their story or their process, as I like to refer to it, only shaped them into what God had created them to be.

True leaders create a barrier against the struggle and persevere against all odds. You are a true leader. Leaders are creative, spontaneous, and unpredictable!

Here are common traits among leaders; do you see yourself in any of these?

- Highly ambitious
- Constant quest for knowledge
- Ability to adapt easily
- Selfless

Leaders understand the importance of being true to who they are. As a leader, you may be tempted to pull back because you don't want to be offensive. You're conscious about letting your light overpower those that aren't shining. The truth is, if you don't walk in the boldness that's on the inside of you, you will live a mediocre life. Leaders will always shine.

# Journal Activity:

Think and reflect on how your story can help lead others to their fearlessness. What leadership qualities do you possess that can help bring change and impact to others?

# Journal Here:

# Faith to Believe

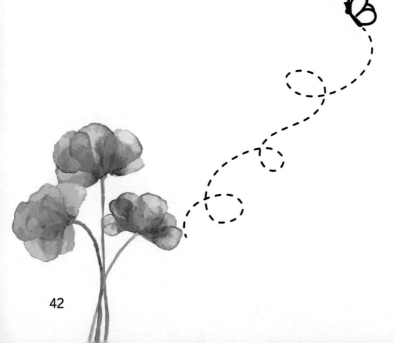

*W*hat if I told you that God wanted you to have everything your heart desires, would you believe me? What if I told you that the reason you have small victories is that you don't really believe you deserve larger victories?

Do you really believe that God is able to do exceedingly abundantly above all that you can ask or think, just like He promised you in His word? Do you know that it takes the same amount of faith to believe for the smaller things as it does for the bigger things? I want you to reflect on that for just a second.

Many people complain about what they don't have but fail to realize that God is not limiting them, they are limiting themselves. There are countless testimonies of people that had great faith and endured the tests to receive an overwhelming blessing. It's easy to applaud the miracles we see in others' lives while we doubt in our hearts that God can and will do the same things for us. If you are waiting for a sign, this is it.

You must increase your faith to live your life full of purpose. Faith in God is where it begins. Faith in His word and what He has promised you is next. Followed by the faith to follow through with what you have been called to do. Faith without works is dead. It's time for you to move.

# Journal Activity:

Think about the areas in your life you have been afraid to explore. Tap into God's word to help you grow in your faith and expand your belief. What scripture can you apply to your faith growth?

# Journal Here:

_____

_____

_____

_____

_____

_____

_____

_____

_____

_____

_____

# Dream Again

$\mathcal{W}$hat is your expectation of your life? Do you find yourself dreaming or have you stopped? Yes, dreams do come true, but you must first have dreams and you must be willing to sacrifice and do the work necessary.

Don't be discouraged with the process. If you have placed your dreams and aspirations on the back burner, it's time to pull them out, dust them off, and put them back on the front of the shelf. Visualize yourself everyday living your dream life. See yourself owning that business, living in that mansion, having a successful family, or traveling around the world.

See yourself impacting lives and being a blessing to others. See it so that you can become it. It's time for you to enlarge your territory and change the course of your family. It's time for you to go big. It's time for you to launch out into the deep and get what you know you have been promised by God. Failure is not an option. Dream on and dream big! It's not your responsibility to know how, it's your responsibility to trust God and believe.

# Journal Activity:

Reflect on your biggest dream. Now write it down. After you have written it down, say this out loud. My dreams of....

_____

_____

_____

_____

_____

_____

are coming to pass.

# Journal Here:

_____

_____

_____

_____

_____

_____

_____

_____

_____

_____

_____

_____

# Speak Up *Louder*

$\mathcal{J}$t's time for you to be heard. There's so much God has placed inside of you and using your voice is critical to your release into a purposeful life. When it comes to living a life of purpose, understanding the value of your voice is very essential to the process. Many women wander through life wondering if what they have to say counts. They wonder if they speak up, will it cause doors to close? Or if they're too honest, will their honesty cause people that they love to leave? They feel that if they are authentic to their voice or authentic to their gift they will be put out of the room.

To live authentically, we must not be afraid to use our voices. When you understand the value and power of your voice, you won't keep silent. You won't be afraid to help others, and you won't be afraid to speak up. When you understand that there is a uniqueness about you, about your talents and your gifts, you'll show up differently in the world.

Others are depending on you to show up, so you must take hold of that responsibility. See yourself as God sees you. Today is a new day. As you build confidence and strength in knowing who you are, think about the value of your voice. Your voice is necessary.

God gave you a unique sound tone and pitch to your voice that no one else has. But He also gave you the ability to turn it on or to turn it off. Today I am giving you your marching orders, it's time for you to turn it on! Your voice is valued, your voice is needed, and your voice is necessary.

# Journal Activity:

Reflect on the times you didn't use your voice to speak. What commitment will you make to use your voice as God intended?

# Journal Here:

_____

_____

_____

_____

_____

_____

_____

_____

_____

_____

_____

_____

# Beauty for *Ashes*

*T*he Bible says you will receive beauty for ashes. Is there any area in your life that needs to be restored? Do you know that your ashes can be turned into something beautiful? What does this mean exactly? It means those things that have been burnt down in your life, He will restore them again. It means the ugly shameful places will soon turn into a place of hope and restoration.

I love it after a rainy day when I can look into the sky and see a rainbow shining so brightly. Even after the worst storms, rainbows emerge. This tells me that although a ravaging storm has hit, and although there may have been destruction, after that process, we can still see God's beauty and His glory. Walking in your purpose brings beauty through the pain. Walking in your purpose, allows you to see the beautiful skyline up ahead.

That's how God works in our lives. He takes those things that man thought would have destroyed us and exchanges them for beauty. The very thing that looks no good or broken, He says, I see beauty. How encouraging is that to know?

There is beauty that is coming out of the pain of your life. There is beauty that is being revealed through your ashes. Today, I want you to think about those areas where there have been ashes, those areas that were meant to destroy you. Now I want you to just take a moment and meditate on the Word of God on the beauty that he is restoring in you today. Once you pursue a life of purpose, you will be unrecognizable. Because you decided to keep going when others said that you should quit, you will experience the beauty of the reward. There will be beauty, there will be restoration, and there will be redemption in your story.

# Journal Activity:

List the areas of your life you want to exchange for more beauty. Release them and give them to God and expect beauty to be your reward.

# Journal Here:

You Are Gifted

*W*hat is it that you love to do? Do you love to sing? Do you love to dance? Do you love to teach?

There's something you love to do that brings you to life. There's something that brings you passion, there's something that brings you joy. Those are your gifts, and it's time for you to explore your great gifts. Most times our gifts start to show in our lives while we are kids. But then as we start 'adulting,' we start putting those things to the side. We start to succumb to the lies that those gifts no longer fit with our lifestyle.

I have to tell you that that's not true. Those things that are your gifts are the things that bring you to life. Those are the things that keep you going and those are the things that bring you closer to your purpose. Living a purposeful life also means a life of fulfillment and joy. It's about experiencing the real essence of who you are.

So today, dust off your gifts. It's time for you to resurrect them. Bring to life those things that you know that you are gifted in. They are the gifts that you're not pursuing right now. Your gifts will make room for you and bring you before great people. You have been gifted to walk this life; your gifts are the reminders. Your gifts are the way God displays that he has touched your life. Not only will your gifts bring life to you, but they will also bring life to others.

# Journal Activity:

Make a list of your gifts and talents. Pick one to reactivate today. Make a new commitment to yourself that you will no longer contain your gifts and you will show up fully the way God made you.

# Journal Here:

_____

_____

_____

_____

_____

_____

_____

_____

_____

_____

_____

Sometimes I don't think that we really understand how important it is for us to tap into our purpose. Let's use the comparison of purpose to an airplane. An airplane generally has a full day schedule to arrive and pick people up by a certain time. But let's say that the airplane gets stuck, or it has engine problems, or the pilot doesn't show up, or the crew doesn't show up for work. How many people will that delay affect? Everything concerning that airplane is on a schedule. One disruption in that schedule can affect hundreds and even thousands of people. A delayed airline can stop a bride from being on time for her wedding. One delayed airplane can stop a business pitch for a multimillion-dollar contract from happening. One delayed flight can cause a mother to miss her child's birthday party or a father from seeing his child being born. A delay can have a domino effect.

It's no different when it comes to your pursuit of purpose. Your delay in living a life in your purpose can affect those you have been destined to impact. There are people that need to hear what you have to say. There are people that need your gifts to help them to birth purpose in their lives.

Don't take your pursuit lightly. Pursue it with vigor. Pursue it with passion. Pursue it with urgency.

Today I want you to have an honest conversation with yourself. Are you pursuing your purpose with urgency or are you being lackadaisical about your pursuit of purpose?

# Journal Activity:

List what mindset shifts you need to make today to pursue your purpose with urgency. What actions can you take starting today to take you to the next level?

# Journal Here:

# Purpose Clues

$\mathcal{K}$nock, Knock, Knock, do you hear that? That's your purpose knocking at your door. It's asking you, "when are you going to show up?" When are you going to be strong? When are you going to be bold? When are you going to make a decision to walk in purpose?

Purpose leaves clues throughout our lives. Purpose shows up in our childhood. Purpose shows up in our teenage years. Purpose shows up in our adult years, and it keeps showing up repeatedly again until we answer the door. Purpose gives us clues to help lead us into becoming the women we were created to be.

Think about this for a moment. What have people said about you or complimented you on throughout your life? These are generally the things that you have done well, or effortlessly. These traits are your purpose clues. Throughout your life, they have been shifting you to walk into the things that you have been called to do.

Today, reflect on your purpose clues. Purpose clues can be anything from awards that you have received in a particular area, or people constantly telling you something about yourself. These are your purpose clues. These are the good traits that I want you to tap into today.

# Journal Activity:

List your purpose clues here. Reflect on the uniqueness of who you are and ask the Holy Spirit to direct you on what you should be doing.

# Journal Here:

_____

_____

_____

_____

_____

_____

_____

_____

_____

_____

_____

_____

# Show Up Queen

$\mathcal{I}$ wasn't until Queen Esther entered the palace that she realized and understood the uniqueness and the responsibility of being God's chosen. As a matter of fact, when the message was first given to her by her uncle, Mordecai, she said that she could be killed if she spoke up to the king without first being called. Her uncle's response to her was, if you don't stand up, there will be another that will rise and take your place. When you are chosen, you have a responsibility to show up. You have a responsibility to take charge. You have the responsibility to take the lead as God's chosen. This means that there are specific assignments that have been made available to you that you must complete. There is a specific thing that you must do as God's chosen.

Being chosen means that out of everyone that God could have put in a position, He selected you. You are chosen because you have what it takes to carry out the mission, whatever that mission may be. If you are in ministry, if you are in the workplace, or if you are in the business world, no matter where you are. You have been elected and selected for the assignment.

Today, I want you to meditate on that. What does it mean to be chosen? And do you really understand the significance of being chosen? Do you value your assignment, or do you complain about it? Do you value the gifts that you have? Or do you wish that you had someone else's? Being chosen is something you should honor. Being chosen is something that you should be thankful for.

Show up, Queen!

# Journal Activity:

Write and reflect on the life assignments you know you have been chosen to carry out. Write a statement of thankfulness and accept the assignment. Decide how you will honor these areas moving forward.

# Journal Here:

# Don't Dim Your Your *Light*

$\mathcal{I}$ once heard this inspiring quote, "go where you're celebrated and not where you are tolerated." When you connect with your purpose tribe, you won't feel the need to dim your light or play small. You won't need to be apologetic about shining in your greatness.

Once you connect with your tribe, you will discover that some people are excited for you to show up and walk into your gift. Don't consume yourself with those that don't want you to show up or don't want you to shine. Focus your attention on the people that want you to be in the room and want to be in the room with you. Some people will also connect with you and celebrate with you. There are also destiny helpers that will come alongside you and help you build your vision. These are the people that will appreciate you for being a gift to the world. When you are walking in your purpose, their voices and faces will be magnified.

Today I want you to reflect on where God is taking you. What rooms is He putting you in? Thank Him in advance for the people that celebrate you. Thank Him for those

that understand and value your gift. Thank Him for the doors that He's opening for you.

You are accepted.

You are loved.

You are needed.

Remove the fear of not being accepted. Remove the fear of people misunderstanding you and thinking that you are acting differently or that you don't deserve the doors that are open for you. There are going to be so many amazing doors that open for you now that you're walking in your purpose. But you have to get over the opinions of others. Your tribe won't be offended by you.

Think about the people that you should be talking to. Think about the people you are going to serve that will appreciate the gift you are to the world. Anything that does not serve your purpose or does not support you and where you're going has to be removed from your environment.

# Journal Activity:

Today, reflect on who needs to be removed from your life that creates unhealthy environments for you. Don't feel guilty if you have outgrown a relationship or a friendship. Thank God for the tribe He has prepared just for you.

# Journal Here:

# Seed Traits

Seed traits are what shape our personality and allow us to fulfill our purpose. They are what define us, such as outgoing, talkative, creative, or eccentric. Seed traits are what you were born with, and they are necessary for your purpose. They mark you with your uniqueness and special gifts. There are hundreds of thousands of people that do what you do, but they can never do it like you. The traits you have, and the way they manifest in your life differentiate you from the rest.

What I love about seed traits is that they allow us to see ourselves the way that God sees us. Seeds grow and blossom into fruit and over time they continue to bear more fruit. What are the seed traits that God has placed in you to fulfill your purpose?

There are specifics about your personality, which are needed for where your purpose is taking you. Satan understands the power and value of our seed traits and will often send someone our way that will destroy our confidence in the very things that make us great. He'll surround us with people that will attempt to belittle or downplay our traits. Sometimes you'll be excommunicated out of groups because your seed traits are seen as a threat instead of valuable. Don't let that deter you.

Be careful not to become ungrateful for how you were created. Your seed traits should not be changed; as a matter of fact, when you try to change yourself to be someone you weren't created to be, you become inauthentic to who God has called us to be. Celebrate the uniqueness of your seed traits.

# Journal Activity:

Write your seed traits below. Reflect on those seed traits that you have been told were negative but should be celebrated. What are those things that you have considered changing about yourself that were really gifts given by God? Seek the Holy Spirit to understand how your seed traits add value to your purpose.

# Journal Here:

_____

_____

_____

_____

_____

_____

_____

_____

_____

_____

_____

# Be Encouraged and Speak *Life*

$\mathcal{T}$abitha reached out to me during one of her darkest moments. She was overwhelmed with everything - her business, her husband, her kids, and her life. She was exhausted and ready to quit, but just as the thoughts of defeat started to play in her head, she began to convince herself that her situation was only temporary. She shifted her environment and looked at herself in the mirror and started to speak the word of God.

"You are the head and not the tail."
(Deuteronomy 28:13)

"You are the lender and not the borrower."
(Deuteronomy 15:16)

"He that is in you is greater than he that is in the world."
(1 John 4:4)

With tears in her eyes, she repeated those words over and over until she felt a calmness come over her and those crazy thoughts started to fade away. What was she doing? She was speaking encouragement to her spirit.

Your thoughts are just as important as the words that come out of your mouth. Well, let's just go a little deeper and say, your thoughts produce the words that come out of your mouth. The Bible tells us in Philippians 4:8 that "whatsoever things are honest" and of a "good report" to think on those things. Why is that? Our life is directly correlated to the things we think. Our thoughts produce our outcomes. How powerful is that! So, whatever you think you become. WOW! When you grasp this concept, it will be a game-changer. Follow this principle to create the life you want. Once you shift your words to faith-filled words of self-encouragement you will produce the life, the lifestyle, the business, the career, or the family you want and deserve.

This is something that you can easily implement into your daily routine. It's the simple things that will create a lifetime of change. If you are having car problems, you may not need to purchase a new car, perhaps you just need to change the water pump. So today let's change your "heart" pump and get the right things feeding to your spirit man. Equip yourself daily with the confessions needed to catapult your life forward. Take time to daily speak confessions out loud to yourself in the mirror, preferably. If you don't have a mirror, no worries, find a quiet place where you can be alone for at least 10 minutes. Take a few deep breaths to calm yourself and keep out the outside distractions.

"Whatever is true, whatever is honorable, whatever is just, whatever is pure, whatever is lovely, whatever is commendable, if there is any excellence, if there is anything worthy of praise, think about these things."
(Philippians 4:8 ESV)

# Journal Activity:

What have you been thinking about yourself? Do your negative thoughts spill over into the words you speak in your life? Speak life into your spirit man daily, by using words of encouragement. What words can you begin to speak out loud to yourself daily? Write the words that will bring life to your purpose and your dreams here.

# Journal Here:

_____

_____

_____

_____

_____

_____

_____

_____

_____

_____

_____

# Anti-Purpose Cycle®

*C*areer, care for others, busy activities, exhaustion, and repeat. This is what I call "the anti-purpose cycle." It is the cycle that keeps you stuck taking the same life course over and over again. It keeps you stuck and on repeat, ultimately causing fatigue and exhaustion. There are so many women stuck in the anti-purpose cycle. It causes them to procrastinate and delay walking in their purpose. They blame their lack of taking action on timing. They blame it on their husbands. They blame it on their children. They blame it on anyone they can, rarely taking the responsibility for their lives.

The cycle keeps many women from fulfilling their purpose. In the anti-purpose cycle, they pretend as if everything is okay. That is not going to be your story. We are not living in the land of pretend. We are living in a land of true fulfillment and true freedom. You may have been stuck in the cycle in the past because you have put the needs of others before yourself. Yes, you should serve others as a part of what God has called you to do but be careful you don't serve others to the detriment of missing your purpose.

Today I want you to make a commitment that you will not allow yourself to be stuck in that cycle any longer. Push and motivate yourself to walk in your purpose with dignity and honor. Work towards the goals that you set for yourself. Dust off those vision boards and life goals that you made for yourself years ago before life started to happen.

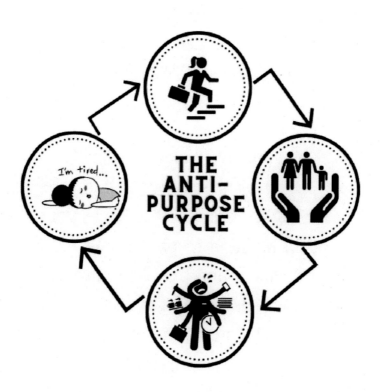

# Journal Activity:

Reflect and write a list of the things that you have allowed to fill your calendar that you know are distractions. Make a commitment that you will not allow those things to keep you out of your purpose any longer.

# Journal Here:

*A*re you ready to be fearless? You have probably heard that word used so many times, but what does it mean? Does it mean that you don't have any fears? Does it mean that nothing causes you to be afraid? Absolutely not. Being fearless does not mean that you don't have fears, it means that you are able to overcome the fears and continue to walk on your path anyways.

I remember when I first started in the business world, I had so many fears. I had fears of failure. I even had fears of success. I had fears of losing my family. I had fears of being perceived as trying to be "too much." There were fears over things that I had not even experienced yet - fear of the unknown.

Fear of the unknown is one common reason for not pursuing our purpose. Many people fear failing or making a wrong decision. What if this isn't my purpose? What if it doesn't work? What if I'm going the wrong way? These are questions most have had when pursuing their purpose.

You're going to have to overcome your fears in order to pursue your purpose. There's no way around it. Be determined to show up big and overcome those fears today. God has not given you the spirit of fear, but of power, love, and a sound mind (2 Timothy 1:7).

Now go, fear less!

# Journal Activity:

Make a list of the things that you are fearful of as it relates to your purpose. What is it that you fear most? After you list those things, make a conscious effort that those things will no longer hinder you.

# Journal Here:

_____

_____

_____

_____

_____

_____

_____

_____

_____

_____

_____

*H*ave you ever thought that you were free from something or someone, only to find out that when they reached out to you, those old emotions were triggered? You thought you were free, but in actuality, you weren't. I can remember a time when I was in bondage to what people thought of me. I wasn't a full-blown "people pleaser," but I always felt like I needed someone to validate that my ideas were good enough before I could step out on anything. My favorite words were, "what do you think about this?" Or "do you think it's a good idea?" I was always explaining my choices to people, instead of making a choice that I really wanted.

I was in bondage to what others thought about me. One day as I was praying, God gave me a revelation. He told me everyone would not understand me, they misunderstood Christ. As long as my heart was pure, my motives were to please Him, and I operated in love, I had nothing to be concerned about. At that moment, I was set free !

God's perfect will for your life, is that you set yourself free from bondage including everything and everyone that

has been holding you back. Freedom is a hard decision for many. Freedom, although it means being free, generally comes with a big cost. The beautiful thing about life is that if you want to experience the God-kind of freedom, it's readily available to you. However, you must be willing to pay the price for it.

What price, you ask? Being really free means you must release yourself from your past and everything you know to be familiar. Walking away from the familiar is a painful experience; it's an emotional separation that few people can really handle. Everyone isn't ready to do that. Freedom requires separation to fully be who God created you to be, without any apologies.

The best gift you can give yourself is the choice of freedom. Freedom allows you to escape from others' views and opinions about your life. Do you struggle with being totally free? Perhaps you're carrying a weight on your shoulders that you aren't even aware of. When you have been broken by the words of others in your past, you can build a wall around your heart and in fact, imprison yourself. You think you're keeping others out, but you're really entrapping yourself. Day-by-day self-realization of the amazingly beautiful woman that you are will ultimately break the bondage.

Your first step is to "give yourself permission to be free." God has already set you free, go ahead and walk in it.

# Journal Activity:

What does freedom mean to you? Write and reflect on the areas in which you have lacked freedom. What actions can you take from today to decrease your fears and increase your faith and live a life of freedom?

# Journal Here:

_____

_____

_____

_____

_____

_____

_____

_____

_____

_____

_____

_____

Day #25

# Living a Purpose-Full *Life*

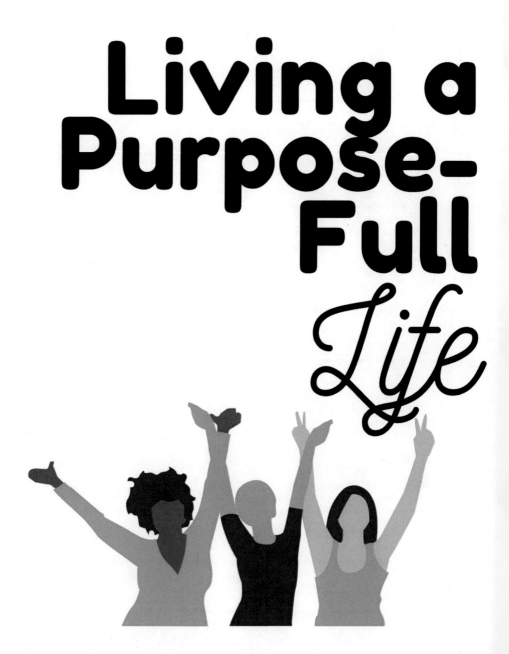

 *P*urpose is defined as "the reason for which something is done or created or for which something exists." Having purpose is the very existence of who you are, the reason that you have been put on this earth. Purpose is also something that so many people seek to find, but many of them rarely find it.

I know you're going to tap into your purpose because you understand who you are. You are beginning to understand the value of your voice. Reflect on your life experiences and what you have learned to bring you to this point. These lessons will help you live a purpose-full life.

Do you know that life change happens with one decision, one commitment, one step, and one dedicated moment? This is your dedicated moment. I have given you the tools to help you bring your purpose to life. Now it's up to you to put it into action. Take it from the journal to full manifestation.

Go ahead and write that book. Start that business. Make that phone call and fill out that application. Go ahead and

enroll in that class. Go ahead and connect with amazing women. Do something today that's going to bring you one step closer to fulfilling your life's purpose. You have your vision, you've written it, and you've made it plain. Now it's the appointed time for you to walk into it.

For everything, there's a time and a season...for this purpose, you were born.

This is your graduation ceremony. This is your elevation in life. Your purpose and your assignment are now showing up so big that you cannot hide it anymore. Purpose has been trying to get your attention. Now you're in a position to listen.

enroll in that class. Go ahead and connect with amazing women. Do something today that's going to bring you one step closer to fulfilling your life's purpose. You have your vision, you've written it, and you've made it plain. Now it's the appointed time for you to walk into it.

For everything, there's a time and a season...for this purpose, you were born.

This is your graduation ceremony. This is your elevation in life. Your purpose and your assignment are now showing up so big that you cannot hide it anymore. Purpose has been trying to get your attention. Now you're in a position to listen.

# Journal Activity:

Think about your life's purpose. What will you do today to live your purpose out loud? What will you do today to bring you closer to walking in your purpose... unapologetically?!

# Journal Here:

_____

_____

_____

_____

_____

_____

_____

_____

_____

_____

_____

_____

# You Can't Lose

*You* can't and you won't lose. This is something I remind myself almost daily. No matter how crazy life's circumstances try to erupt around you, don't allow them to shift your belief. Paul said in Philippians 4:11 that no matter what state he was in, he had learned to be content. Make that the standard for your life. When you know you can't lose, you act accordingly. As you commit to live a life of purpose, things will not always be easy. In fact, the more absolute you are about living a life of purpose, the more storms will rage. But keep this in mind.

You can feel amazing, no matter what. Why? Because feeling amazing is not predicated on any external factors, it is all internal. It's a feeling you can choose to live in all day, every day...No matter what.

- Keep feeling amazing even when the walls around you are falling apart.
- Keep feeling amazing even when you feel disappointed.
- Keep feeling amazing even when people leave your life.
- Keep feeling amazing even when things don't go your way.

# Journal Activity:

Think about a time when things didn't go as planned. Now that you know you can't lose, how will you handle yourself next time? How will you respond to life's challenges?

# Journal Here:

_____

_____

_____

_____

_____

_____

_____

_____

_____

_____

_____

# Do It
## Afroid

*I* remember planning for my first big talk in front of an audience of college students and their parents. This was the first time I was introduced as a motivational speaker and to say I was nervous was an understatement. My fears told me to cancel at least three times, because "I wasn't ready." I attempted to write my presentation but found myself constantly ripping it up and starting over. The day finally came and with just a few bullet points scratched in my notebook, I delivered my speech.

That night as I stood with the microphone in my hand and began speaking from my heart, there was a breakthrough that hit the room. The speech ended in a standing ovation. I wish I could take the credit, but I was a vessel used by God. I showed up and delivered, although I was afraid.

That was over seven years ago, and I have been standing and speaking in front of rooms since that day. Life has a way of pushing us to our purpose even when we feel we aren't ready. The truth is, we are. This is why I am passionate about helping women unlock their purpose because I know once they do, they will become unstoppable.

While you are on the discovery to purpose, I want you to accept your purpose and soar. Focus on the things that really matter and remove any distractions that keep you from soaring. When things become difficult, press through them. Do it afraid.

Challenge yourself to reach higher heights. Be determined to leave your legacy in this world. Always remember that your purpose was given to you before you were formed. It belongs to you, and no one can stop you from pursuing it.

# Journal Activity:

What do you need to do although you are afraid? Write about it on the next page.

Fill in the blank.
I will not allow my fear of _____
to keep me from walking in my purpose.

# Journal Here:

_____

_____

_____

_____

_____

_____

_____

_____

_____

_____

_____

_____

Shine
Bright
Like a
*Diamond*

*A*s far back as the Garden of Eden, there has been a fight to shift our identity. Being tricked out of our rightful place isn't anything new. It's the oldest trick of Satan to shake up God's plan to destroy the purpose that God has for mankind. It started when the serpent spoke to Eve and convinced her that she didn't hear what she actually heard and caused her to doubt if what God gave her was really enough. We know how the story ends; the questioning or doubting ultimately led to her and Adam being kicked out of the garden.

There are so many people living beneath the standards that have been set for their life because they don't know who they are. The enemy has tried to limit them from shining because he knows their destiny is tied to their ability to shine. How do we shine? We shine by walking in our purpose. We shine by helping others to discover their destiny. We don't shine in obscure or dark places.

When you shine so bright, there is nothing that will be able to hide you. When you shine brightly you will become a lighthouse for others to find their way. The enemy will try to trick you into believing that your light isn't necessary. If this were true, then God would not have mentioned to us to be the light so many times throughout the Word of God.

Walk boldly in your purpose and shine bright like the diamond that you are.

# Journal Activity:

Has the enemy tricked you out of your rightful place? Has he stolen your identity? What can you do today to get back on the right path?

# Journal Here:

# The Beauty of the Journey

*T*he day you realize your purpose and see yourself as you truly are, will be the day you change this world. If I had a chance to speak to my younger self, I would tell her...

Things aren't as bad as they seem.

Tomorrow will be brighter.

You can't fail.

You're forgiven and you don't need to walk in guilt.

You can have the life you dreamed about.

You can have it all, you don't have to choose.

Anything you don't like, change it.

You are the only one responsible for the life you live.

You will be "too much" for some people and that's okay. Stay true to your authentic self.

I am sure you can attest that as you grow, learn and reflect, you will recognize that you're so much more than you give yourself credit for. There is a world that is waiting for you to walk in your purpose...don't keep them waiting.

# Journal Activity:

What words of wisdom would you give to your younger self? What has life taught you? Write it down and reflect on the beauty of the journey.

# Journal Here:

$\mathcal{I}$ had a wonderful, engaging lady contact me about scheduling a free coaching consultation. She was excited, and definitely ready to take her life to the next level. We talked for almost 45 minutes about how many degrees she had earned, the large corporations she led, the projects she managed, and the numerous social and political groups she was an active member of. We went on to discuss how she had been wanting to start her own business for the past 15 years but had allowed herself to be limited by her fear of failure. I listened as she talked.

I've heard "her story" so many times from so many women that were well-qualified and should be overly confident in their natural God-given abilities. As the conversation went on further, she said, "I know what I need to do to launch my first conference, but what if no one shows up?" She admitted to me that she was afraid of failing.

I won't go much deeper into what I told her, but I will say this. She felt energized, and excited after our talk and she said, "I'm ready to get started." Sadly, I never heard from her again.

You see for years, 15 years to be exact, she had been self-sabotaging and talking herself out of her dreams. She had promoted others and their businesses and hid behind the "strong-supporter role" that so many women hide behind. It's a crutch that keeps women stuck from stepping out into their destiny. Although I could help lead her to the life she dreamed of, she had to be the one to decide that she really wanted it.

She had to make the shift necessary to experience her next level. Today you have to make the same decision. You have to accept that you're worth more and you won't settle by staying in your comfort zone.

# Journal Activity:

Reflect and write about the shift you need to make to live a fearless life of purpose.

# Journal Here:

_____

_____

_____

_____

_____

_____

_____

_____

_____

_____

_____

_____

# Day #31

# You Made It

When I was a little girl, I remember a song called "Livin' For The Weekend" by The O'Jays. It's one of those classics that still resonates with me just a bit. When I worked in corporate America, we used to "live for the weekends." We were trained to believe that Fridays meant time off, although life doesn't slow down on the weekend. In fact, life kicks up a few gears.

Allow me to step on your toes for just a bit. Are you living for the weekends, for the paycheck or are you living out your purpose? I want to challenge you today to live for something so much more than just your weekends. I have been in quiet reflection thinking about "my 2016." That year I lost both my grandmothers within 2 months of each other; launched my first tour (on a wing and a prayer); published my first book; received recognition from a U.S. Congresswoman for my work in the community; lost some friends; made some new ones; shed some tears and still, despite of it all (good and bad), I jumped up every day ready to impact the world.

I made it, and so will you! Are you ready to live your fearless life of purpose? You've listened to enough teachings, attended enough seminars, read enough books, and subscribed to enough motivational gurus. Make a decision and take one step today toward your dreams! You have what it takes. You have nothing to lose!

DREAM, DREAM, DREAM...DO, DO, DO!

I love you and I'm praying for you.

# Journal Activity:

Reflect on your past 30-day journey. Write about what you have learned about yourself. What do you need to do to live your best life?

# Journal Here:

_____

_____

_____

_____

_____

_____

_____

_____

_____

_____

_____

_____

# monthly goals

## January

- _____
- _____
- _____

## February

- _____
- _____
- _____

## March

_____

_____

_____

# monthly goals

## April

- 
- 
- 

## May

- 
- 
- 

## June

- 
- 
-

# monthly goals

## July

- _____
- _____
- _____

## August

- _____
- _____
- _____

## September

_____

_____

_____

# monthly goals

## October

- _____
- _____
- _____

## November

- _____
- _____
- _____

## December

- _____
- _____
- _____